EVEN PRESIDENTS

WANT TO KNOW IF THEY ARE GOING TO

HEAVEN

How to Be Sure You Are Going to Heaven

Patricia Palmer White

ISBN 978-1-63885-683-2 (Paperback)
ISBN 978-1-63885-684-9 (Digital)

Copyright © 2022 Patricia Palmer White
All rights reserved
First Edition

Scripture taken from the Holy Bible New International
Version, unless otherwise indicated
Copyright 1973, 1978, 1984, International Bible Society.
Used by permission of Zondervan Bible Publishers.
Patricia Palmer White
© 2011
Scripture identified KJV is from the King
James Version of the Bible.
Photo by Keith Williams, two-time Pulitzer
Prize-winning photojournalist.

Covenant Books
11661 Hwy 707
Murrells Inlet, SC 29576
www.covenantbooks.com

DEDICATION

This book is dedicated to my late husband, Rev. Calvin D. White, pastor of the Beargrass Missionary Baptist Church in Louisville, Kentucky, for eighteen years and the Union Bethel Baptist Church in Chesapeake, Virginia, for seven years until the Lord called him home to be with Him. The Lord blessed me with fifty wonderful years of marriage to this man of God whose solid faith and unwavering commitment to teaching and preaching an uncompromising gospel of Jesus Christ taught me what it meant to have patience and a good sense of humor. I miss his laughter that permeated the premises; no matter where he was, you knew he was there. The Book of Hebrews tells us that Jesus was anointed with the oil of joy. I believe Calvin was anointed also with the oil of joy.

CONTENTS

ACKNOWLEDGEMENTS

To my mother, Ellen Palmer, and my mother-in-law, Lucille White (both lived ninety-nine years), whose quiet spirit was a testimony to those who knew them.

To my friend Rev. Linda Gazaway, my Barnabas, who with me studied, cried, laughed, shared, and celebrated the good news of Jesus Christ.

To my niece, Leonette Leavell, who introduced me to the Bible study program that started me on my personal journey with Jesus.

To my granddaughter, Kevina, in whom I have seen the first seed of faith I planted morph into a beautiful woman of God.

To my wonderful daughter, Jaci, who helped me research this book and kept me focused, and whose genuine love and compassion for people has made me a better person.

To my son, Rev. Kevin W. White, who since childhood has endured numerous surgeries yet persevered to the doctorate program at Southern Baptist Seminary, for our long discussions and his insightful comments.

To Rev. Charles H. Duncan, the esteemed pastor of the historical Virginia Avenue Baptist Church, Louisville, Kentucky, and former professor at Simmons Bible College, whose profound teachings gave me an insatiable appetite for the Word of God.

To my friend Veronda Deloatch for her patience and computer knowledge that helped take this from man-uscript to book. I am so grateful for her dedication and commitment.

To my many friends, family, church family and the many others who have blessed my life and influenced my spiritual direction in such positive ways, I say thank you for your love and support. Most of all, I thank God for Jesus who is my Savior and my ever-present friend.

INTRODUCTION

My mom and dad were Baptist. My dad's father was one of the founders of the Men's Star Bible Class at his church, where my dad became active. He loved the Men's Star Bible Class, where he taught Bible study. My mom had sick babies but always saw to it that my sister and I went to a Baptist church close by within walking distance. I remember being very young and holding hands as we walked to church. At that time, Mom was not able to attend church, but I would often see her reading her devotional and kneeling to pray. When we started grade school, all the kids in our project would walk together to a nearby Catholic Church and to their summer camps and programs. At age twelve, I joined the Catholic Church along with my sister and my friends. The fact that we had broken a long-held tradition of being a Baptist family did not bother Mom and Dad one bit, as long as we were in church. After all, we are all serving the same God with our eyes on the same destination—heaven. I did not know Jesus then, but I knew all about the Virgin Mary and St. Jude.

After two years of college, I dropped out. I was working for the Treasury Department in Washington, DC, when I married this handsome sailor I had met and dated years ago while in high school. Calvin White and I married in the Catholic Church, and he agreed that we would raise our children in the Catholic faith. This good-looking guy had something about him that was special. We moved to his hometown, Louisville, Kentucky, and there I found that I had married into a lovely Christian family of five boys and three girls. This was a large family compared to mine, and we used to all have Sunday dinner at his parents' and spend the whole day together in laughter and fun. Mrs. White was a homemaker and an excellent cook. Mr. White was a hard worker and a disciplinarian, and all his kids, both sons and daughters, were taught to clean, cook, and work. On Sundays, it was Sunday school, church, and back to church at 6:00 p.m. for BTU. He was a good, fun kind of man, but he did not spare the rod and spoil the child. All his children grew to be successful, and they all loved the Lord.

Calvin and I started our family, raising our son and daughter in the Catholic Church as planned.

Calvin worked as a firefighter for the Louisville Fire Department, and I as a clerk typist for the Naval Ordnance Plant. Every Sunday morning, we went our separate ways. Very active in his childhood church, Calvin continued to worship there, and the children and I went to the Catholic Church in our neighborhood where I became the youth director. There were a lot of changes being made in the Catholic Church at that time, and I was beginning to lose interest. At Calvin's church, things were at a standstill, so we decided to search for a place to worship together as a family.

This decision led us to the Beargrass Missionary Baptist Church pastored by Calvin's childhood friend, Rev. Charles Henry Duncan. This was the turning point in my Christian walk for it was there that I met Jesus.

The four of us joined Beargrass and immediately began to study, work, and serve. Our children went to Sunday school and joined the choir and the youth group, where I became the director. My husband taught Sunday school, sang in the choir, became a trustee and, later, a deacon. But most importantly, we went to Wednesday-night Bible study, and there I was introduced to the beautiful Word of God, the most fascinating book in the entire world—the Bible. The most memorable thing that comes to mind during that time was when I asked Rev. Duncan, "Who are these children of Israel that you keep talking about?" After a chuckle and a few laughs, the pastor explained that they were not laughing at me and for me to keep asking questions because that is how you learn. And learn I did. The more I learned, the more I wanted to know. That led me to Simmons Bible College (now Simmons University), where Rev. Duncan taught the Old and New Testament. I convinced my best friend, Linda, to go with me, and together we started on our journey of faith.

My friend Linda and I were so eager to learn all we could about our Lord, we were constantly looking for the next Bible study. My niece, Leonette, fondly called Boo, told us about the Bible Study Fellowship (BSF) that was held all around the world at certain churches. Sure enough, we found a church in Louisville, and we completed all the studies they had to offer at the time.

Searching for the next good, sound Bible study, Linda's friend told her about Precepts Bible Study. Each study was more in depth and more intense, with lots of homework and researching the Greek and Hebrew text. We were soaking it all up. I had no idea the Bible was so interesting. Linda took the course to become a Precepts teacher and started classes at our church. She is now an ordained minister at our church. I did not quite go that far, but God blessed me with a love for teaching youth. I began teaching youth Bible study, Sunday school, Vacation Bible School, etc., and I loved it. As I studied to teach, I grew deeper and deeper in love with Jesus. It helped me develop my relationship with Jesus and helped me later in my calling as a pastor's wife and first lady.

As I grew in my Christian walk, I was also growing in my job with the federal government. As a wage and classification specialist, it was an exceptionally good job with excellent pay and benefits, but I was not happy. Those were the worst of years and the best of years—the worst because I was crushed and brought to my knees; the best because that was when I first recognized God and heard Him speak to me. Although I gave off the persona of a confident Black woman who walked tall and held her head up high, my insides were screaming for a way out. I could not stand the pressure of that job. I had to make decisions about people's pay grade and their salaries. A meeting had been scheduled for me to address the concerns of some disgruntled employees, their union representative, and the head of the department. They had a complaint about their pay grade.

As I headed to lunch that day, I had made up my mind that I was going home and going to call in sick. There was no way I was going to face that angry group that day. On my way home on the expressway, I heard a voice say, "Turn around, Lo, I am with you always." It was not an audible voice, but I heard it anyway, loud and clear, as it spoke to me the same words, over and over again, as I continued to drive. I recognized those words, *Lo, I am with you always*, as

God's words in the Bible. Finally, at the next exit, I found myself swerving to get off the expressway and head back to work. All I remembered was walking into that room as confident as anyone could possibly be.

I took charge of that meeting, or should I say the Lord took charge of that meeting, and not a soul challenged me. Of course, they filed an appeal, but I won the appeal. As I read the appeal and my classification rationale in the evaluation statement, I knew that God had to have helped me write it. And He has been right here with me ever since in everything I do.

After twenty-five years of government service and doctor's appointments for depression, I resigned. I needed only five more years to take an early retirement. But I could not take another five years in that job. In retrospect, I now realize that it was God making me uncomfortable. He knew it would take a lot to make me quit my "good government job," as I used to refer to it. We had just bought a new home, and our daughter was in college; quitting that job was not an option. But as always, God made a way. Little did I know at the time that God would use this to draw me closer to Him. I wanted to know all about Him and His Son. Jesus became my best friend and my focus. I began to realize if I just kept my focus on Him, Jesus would be true to His promises.

In the meantime, at our church, Calvin had announced his call to the ministry and enrolled in school. He received his master's in religious education, and when our pastor answered the call to another church, Calvin was called to pastor our church. After eighteen years as pastor of the Beargrass Missionary Baptist Church, we relocated to Virginia, and he served seven years as pastor of the Union Bethel Baptist Church in Chesapeake until the Lord called him home June 2, 2011.

More and more, I could hear Jesus speaking to me or redirecting me when I was getting off track. I concentrated on making it a habit to spend time every morning in His Word and in prayer. What started out to be five or ten minutes with God would sometimes turn out to be an hour or more. I started keeping a journal of the many incidents I recognized as God working in my life. I was getting bolder and bolder in my witness. I began to understand why my husband was so content and let nothing bother him. His favorite hymn was "It Is Well with My Soul." When he died, God showed me the scripture in Isaiah 46:4 (NIV): "Even to your old age and gray hair, I am He who will sustain you, I have made you and I will carry you; I will sustain you, and I will rescue you." It was God letting me know that I had nothing to fear because He would always be there for me. I have claimed that scripture many times, and God has not failed me yet.

I want to mention specifically when the bank was putting my home into foreclosure, and I had received the notification from the bank's attorney, my friend warned me that I should immediately start putting in applications for apartments because it was harder to get accepted when you were going through a foreclosure. Immediately, God reminded me of Isaiah 46:4 and His promise to me. I told my friend absolutely not because I would be telling God that I did not trust Him to keep His word, and I know His promises are true. I did not know how He was going to do it because the situation looked bleak, but I knew He would, and He did, and I am still in my home today. This is only one of the many times that God has intervened for me, but each time, I trusted He would. And that is the key—trust. You have got to trust that He is going to do what He says He will do. As the popular sign goes, TRUST GOD NO MATTER WHAT.

I would always say how much I wished others knew Jesus like I know Him. There is so much fear and hatred in the world, people taking their own life or the lives of others. I kept thinking, if only they knew Jesus and knew how simple it is to know Him in the forgiveness of their sins. People just do not know what they are missing, the peace and joy in just knowing Him. There are people who think that there is no hope, but I want them to know that there is hope and where and how to find it. Then God began speaking to me about writing a book. I know it was God because me writing a book is just out of the question. I have an extremely limited vocabulary, and my command of the English language is terrible. Over and over, God kept speaking to me in various ways. I would read a magazine or book that would get my attention about writing. I would see a program on TV, or someone would just off the cuff start talking about writing a book. It was weird, but there were many instances and reminders about the book.

When I protested about my lack of knowledge or ability and that I had no formal degree, God told me that was exactly why He was using me. He wanted this book to be written in layman's language, easy to understand, clear and concise and simple to read. He wanted it to be user-friendly, free of big words and theological terminology. He wanted anybody to be able to pick up this book and not be intimidated by it, a book that even a child could understand if read to him. After all, in the Bible, Jesus says, "Truly I tell you, unless you change and become like little children, you cannot enter the kingdom of heaven" (Matt. 18:3 NIV). Jesus is telling us to be trusting and have faith like a child.

For four years, I tried to run from this responsibility that I felt God had given me. I knew that I was being disobedient, so I tried to rationalize, saying perhaps that it was not God calling me to write this book. I finally accepted this calling because I knew if God called me, He would equip me. He would show me what to do and tell me what to say. And guess what? He has done just that.

My prayer is that this book and the quoted scriptures will prove that the way to heaven is not complicated. That you will experience the joy and peace that comes only in knowing that you can never do enough, and you can never be good enough. Only Jesus is enough. His grace is sufficient: "For it is by grace you have been saved, through faith—and this not from yourselves, it is the gift of God—not by works, so that no one can boast" (Eph. 2:8–9). Thank God for Jesus!

CHAPTER 1

Heaven or Hell
(THE CHOICE IS YOURS)

Steve Jobs, visionary founder and CEO of Apple Computers, said, "No one wants to die. Even people who want to go to heaven don't want to die to get there. And yet, death is a destination we all share." The Bible tells us many things about death. Ecclesiastes 7:2 (NIV) tells us, "Death is the destiny of every man; the living should take this to heart." A No. 1 *New York Times* best-selling author Mitch Albom wrote *Tuesdays with Morrie*, a memoir about his friend, Morrie, who was dying of ALS. Morrie tells him, "Everybody knows they're going to die, but nobody believes it. If we did, we would do things differently."

Do you believe you are going to die? If so, has it influenced how you live? If you believed death was imminent, what would you do? The Bible makes it clear in Hebrews 9:27 that "it is appointed unto man once to die then the judgment." Romans 5:12 and 1 Corinthians 15:22 explains why man must die and tells us that death entered the world through one man (Adam) and through him passed to all people. In other words, because of Adam's sin of disobedience in the garden of Eden, all mankind has been condemned to die. The Bible states in Romans 6:23, "For the wages of sin is death…" Adam sinned against God, and because of Adam, we are all born with a death sentence. And death is not a respecter of persons; it matters not if you are rich or poor, famous or unknown, Black or white, the pope or an atheist, Jewish or Islamic. We are all going to die one day, and that is a fact that cannot be denied. The question is, are we prepared to die, and what is after death?

The Bible also tells us there is a heaven and there is a hell. The Pew Research Center's 2014 Religious Landscape Study reported roughly 72 percent of Americans believe in heaven. There have been claims of people who have died, gone to heaven, and come back to tell what it is like. There have been books written and TV specials on the subject such, as the December 20, 2005, Barbara Walters television special *Heaven: Where Is Heaven? How do We Get There?* There have been several movies, one of which is a story, *Heaven Is for Real*, based on a Midwestern pastor whose son claims to have visited heaven during a near-death experience. There have been songs written about heaven—"Everybody Talking about Heaven Ain't Going There" pretty much sums it all up, as does Scripture when Jesus said in Matthew 7:21, "Not everyone who says to me, 'Lord, Lord,' will enter the kingdom of heaven." So who is going to heaven and how do they get there? Are you one of the many people searching for the answer?

People have pondered the mysteries of heaven for years, wondering how to get there. Some of the most powerful people are still not sure of their destiny after life. The most sought-after answer most human beings long to know is the answer to the question, "How do I know if I am going to heaven?" An evangelist named John Townsend answered the question for Queen Victoria of the UK when she asked, "Can one be absolutely sure in this life of eternal safety?" He referred her to the following passages of Scripture: John 3:16 and Romans 10:9–10. After she discovered the assurance of salvation through faith in Christ, the Queen of England surrendered her life to Christ and started carrying copies of a small booklet concerning the plan of salvation to give to her subjects.

Everybody wants to go to heaven, but no one wants to die to get there. Why is that? Do you think maybe they are afraid of death, or is it because they are not so sure whether they are going to heaven or hell? Wow!

Even presidents are asking the question, "How do I know if I am going to heaven?" In an article published in the August 20, 2007, issue of *Time* magazine, an excerpt from a book by Nancy Gibbs and Michael Duffy describes how previous presidents often asked that question of the prolific preacher Dr. Billy Graham:

> Back in 1955 when Dwight Eisenhower had become Graham's first real friend in the White House, he used to press the evangelist on how people can really know if they are going to heaven.
>
> John F. Kennedy wanted to talk about how the world would end—more than an abstract conversation for the first generation of Presidents who had the ability to make that happen.
>
> Lyndon Johnson was obsessed with his own mortality... The President even scripted his own exit. One day Johnson took Graham on a walk around his Texas ranch, to a clearing in the trees near where his parents were buried. Johnson wanted to know if he would see them again in heaven. And then another question:

"Would Billy preach at his funeral?" ... "I want you to look in those cameras and just tell 'em what Christianity is all about. Tell 'em how they can be sure they can go to heaven. I want you to preach the gospel."

When he got home, Graham wrote to Johnson, expressing his love and reassurance, in case Johnson still had any doubts. "We are not saved because of our accomplishments," Graham reminded the President. "I am not going to heaven because I have preached to great crowds or read the Bible many times. I'm going to heaven just like the thief on the cross who said in that last moment: 'Lord, remember me.'" (Adapted from *The Preacher and the Presidents*, Thorndike Press: 2008)

Evangelist Arthur Blessitt, famous for having carried a twelve-foot cross around the world, details on his website his experience and his meeting with George W. Bush. Mr. Bush, then a Texas oilman and son of Vice-President George H. Bush, heard Mr. Blessitt on a radio broadcast preaching at a Midland, Texas, meeting called Decision 84. Mr. Bush asked one of his friends to arrange a meeting with Blessitt so he could talk to him about Jesus. Blessitt describes how Mr. Bush looked him in the eyes with a calm, steady look and said, "I want to talk to you about Jesus Christ and how to follow Him." Blessitt asked Mr. Bush that if he died this moment, would he have the assurance that he would go to heaven? George Bush replied no. Arthur Blessitt then explained how he could have that assurance and helped the future President George W. Bush to accept Jesus. Mr. Blessitt wrote, "A good and powerful day. Led Vice-President Bush's son to Jesus today. George Bush Jr.! This is great! Glory to God."

Are you plagued with the question, "How do I know if I am going to heaven?" Nine out of ten people believe in heaven, but very few are sure they are going there. Are you one of those people in doubt? The Bible tells you not only whether you are saved and going to heaven but also how to be sure of your salvation and your destination. You should know, and only you and God know if you are going to heaven. I may say I am saved, I may have joined church and been baptized, I may quote scripture and even act like I'm saved, I may teach Bible Study and do all the right things to project that I am saved, but no one knows if I am truly saved except me and God. It is a personal thing, for only God can read the heart. But if you know beyond a shadow of doubt that you are saved and going to spend eternity in heaven with God, that is all that matters. But if you are not sure and are still on a soul-searching journey for peace and contentment, and if you cannot answer yes with confidence, then you are utterly lost, my friend. But if you know in whom you believe, no matter what comes your way, you will have that blessed assurance that surpasses all understanding.

In the legendary Whitney Houston's last interview with Diane Sawyer, Diane asked her about her lifestyle and persisted in questioning Whitney concerning her drug abuse, her abusive marriage to Bobby Brown, and other negative things in her life. Whitney Houston patiently answered each question, then she threw her head back and, with a smile on her face, said with conviction, "I know one thing. Jesus loves me." Do you have that assurance that Jesus loves you, or are you one of those people in doubt? Do you answer, "I think so" or "I hope so"? Or do you answer with confidence, with a resounding, "YES, I KNOW SO"? As Diane continued to question Whitney about embarrassing moments in her life, Whitney Houston never lost sight of the unconditional love Jesus has for her. Romans 8:1–2 says, "[T]here is no condemnation for those who are in Christ Jesus because through Christ Jesus the law of the Spirit of Life set me free from the law of sin and death." Whitney knew that, and that is why she was able to smile.

She knew she had a Savior who loved her in spite of her, and she was confident He would do what He promised. Are you as convinced as Whitney was that nothing can separate you from His love?

God wants you too to be sure of your salvation. You will never have peace in your life until you are sure of what will happen to you after this life. Until you have that blessed assurance of heaven, you will always be searching for something that is missing in your life. In John 4:18, the Samaritan woman at the well had been searching for love. She had been married five times and was presently living with a man and was still unfulfilled. Until she met Jesus. Many people try to satisfy their emptiness, realizing that something is missing but not knowing what it is because their life is void of Jesus. An endless pursuit of things leaves them empty and hollow and broken inside; things that can never satisfy. They have an emptiness that only God can fill. People attempt to satisfy their yearning with relationships and other involvements. They end up experiencing only disappointment. People are still searching and looking in all the wrong places. Some look for happiness in money or fame, in sex or drugs, in gangs or cults, in jobs or hobbies, and on the Internet, but until you find happiness in Jesus Christ, you will always be searching. All these things offer false fulfillment. Lasting happiness can only be found in one Person—Jesus. Only then will you have peace with God.

There will always be a void in your life. King Solomon, the wisest and richest king in all of Israel, wrote in Ecclesiastes that life without God is empty of purpose and meaning. He had tried everything under the sun to find happiness. In the whole book of Ecclesiastes, you find King Solomon searching, and after achieving everything from friends to fortune and fame, he concluded in the last two verses of Ecclesiastes, "Now all has been heard; here is the conclusion of the matter: Fear God and keep His commandments, for this is the whole duty of man. For God will bring every deed into judgment, including every hidden thing, whether it is good or evil" (Eccl. 12:13–14).

Many people go through life feeling empty, inadequate, and unworthy. Our attempt at happiness often leaves us hopeless and yearning for fulfillment. You may feel unworthy of God's love, but there is nothing you have done or can do that will keep God from loving you. You do not have to live life with a feeling of hopelessness. St. Augustine had desperately searched for fulfillment in excessive pleasures, false religions, and philosophy until he found his peace with God and was baptized. It was then he wrote, "You have made us for yourself, O Lord, and our heart is restless until it rests in you." God has a purpose for your life, and

He does not want you to be lonely, afraid, or rejected. He wants you to feel loved, and He wants to give you that joy and peace that can only be found in His Son, Jesus Christ. He wants you to be so full of His love that you will want to shout it from the rooftop, and you will want to share Him with others so they too will know this wonderful feeling of knowing that you are forever safe for all eternity. In the Bible, Ecclesiastes 3:11 states that God has set eternity in the human heart. In other words, God has given man a desire for eternity so he can never be satisfied with what is temporary. This life is temporary, and man knows it. He will never find true happiness in this world. True happiness apart from Christ is impossible.

Tyler Perry summed it all up when he quoted Romans 8:38–39 (KJV) at Whitney Houston's funeral:

> For I am persuaded, that neither death, nor life, nor angels, nor principalities, nor powers, nor things present, nor things to come, nor height, nor depth, nor any other creature, shall be able to separate us from the love of God, which is in Christ Jesus our Lord.

I do not know where Whitney Houston is; that is between her and God. But I do believe she is in heaven. Are you fully persuaded of your destination? Is it heaven or hell? Only you can answer that question.

CHAPTER 2

Too Good to Be True
(IT'S SO SIMPLE THAT YOU MISS IT)

God has made access to heaven so simple, most people miss it. You have heard the saying, "If it's too good to be true, it probably is." Well, that statement does not apply to salvation. To the contrary, God has made it so simple to get to heaven that most people just cannot fathom it. They believe there must be more to it. They believe they have got to do something, anything—say ten Hail Marys, bow down three times a day, fast, do good deeds, have good karma, keep holy days, perform rituals, adhere to tradition, have high moral and ethical standards, keep all the sacraments of the church, and the list goes on and on. It is just human nature to want to do something to receive something in return, even salvation. I need to work for it, pay for it, etc.

In the Bible, 2 Kings chapter 5 tells of Naaman, the commander of the army of Aram, who had leprosy and was advised of a prophet of the Lord named Elisha, who could cure him of his leprosy.

When the prophet sent word to Naaman to just wash himself seven times in the Jordan River to be cured, Naaman became indignant. He wanted the Prophet Elisha to come to him and stand and call on the name of the Lord his God, wave his hand over the spot, and cure him of his leprosy. Naaman's servant said to him, "Master, if the prophet had told you to do some great thing, would you not have done it?" The servant knew that his master would have paid any price and done any difficult task demanded by the prophet, so why not just do the simple thing he suggested? It was just too good to be true. It was too simple to wash seven times in the Jordan. There just had to be more to it than that. Besides, why did he have to come to Israel to bathe in the Jordan when the waters of Damascus were better?

Naaman finally relented and did as the prophet had told him, and the Bible says his flesh was restored and became clean like that of a young boy. Naaman was so excited and filled with a heart of thanksgiving he acknowledged faith in Elisha's God. Naaman wanted to pay Elisha, but the prophet informed the commander that payment could not be accepted. You cannot pay God for His blessing of healing. Salvation, both deliverance and healing, is free by God's grace alone. Ephesians 2:8–9 says, "For it is by grace you have been saved, through faith, and not of yourselves; it is the gift of God, not by works, so that no one can boast." When Naaman acknowledged faith in God, he had not only been healed but saved by faith.

Just like Naaman could not believe that all he had to do was dip in the Jordan River seven times to be cured of leprosy, there are people today who find it hard to believe that they do not have to do anything, pay anything, or work for anything in order to go to heaven. God loves you so much He gave His Son Jesus to die that you might live in all eternity in heaven with Him. You cannot do anything to make God love you, and you cannot do anything to make God not love you. He loves you anyway, unconditionally, just the way you are—filthy, sinful, and all messed up. All God really wants is for you to know and love His Son. All He asks is that you admit you are a sinner, that you need a Savior, and that you are willing to turn from your sinful ways and follow Jesus.

Christian Picciolini had spent eight years in the white supremacist movement. No longer a white supremacist, he now spends his time trying to help pull people out of the movement. Picciolini said, looking back, he describes his introduction to the group as receiving a "lifeline of acceptance." It is tough to find something to believe in. Today, people are still joining gangs and cults, trying to find something to believe in. The climate is right. People are searching and yearning to satisfy an inner desire. There are books, movies, documentaries; there are religious theme parks, such as the Creation Museum, the Ark Encounter, and the Holy Land Experience. Today, we have artists and athletes who are rich and famous but poor in spirit because they are still unhappy and unfulfilled. They are still searching for something to satisfy that void in their life. They consult mediums, psychics, astrology, and all the New Age technology, spending money on the latest divination practices, hoping to find peace. Their hope still lies in worldly things.

Ray C. Stedman, in his book *God's Final Word*, tells of Rev. Billy Graham being invited to the home of Sir Winston Churchill, the Prime Minister of England. Churchill asked Rev. Graham, "Can you give an old man any hope?" Rev. Graham took his pocket New Testament and told Churchill that "the Bible offers not only hope to the world in the ultimate triumph of Jesus Christ but hope for individual human beings in the plan of salvation." Just like the prime minister, millions of people today struggle with that same question. Can anyone offer the human race any hope?

Do you believe if you go to church every Sunday and tithe, you will go to heaven? Or if you love everybody and try to live by the golden rule of "Do unto others as you would have them do unto you," that will get you into heaven? Do you believe that your pastor or your priest has a better chance of getting into heaven than you do, or that they are closer to God than you are? Well, that is not true. We all have direct access to God through Jesus Christ, and we all get into heaven the same way, by faith in Jesus Christ.

Do you think that you have done such awful things in your life that there is no way you could possibly get to heaven? You can get to heaven no matter how bad your sin is. In Matthew 9:13 (KJV), Jesus said, "For I am not come to call the righteous, but sinners to repentance." The Bible further states in Luke 19:10 (KJV), "For the Son of Man is come to seek and to save that which was lost." That means you and me. No matter how hard you try, do you find it difficult to forgive yourself? When you try to do right, does it seem like you always fail? Welcome to humanity. You are not alone.

Sometimes when sharing the gospel, we make it more complicated than it needs to be. It may sound complex, but it is not. The Bible has a simple story. God made man. Man rejected God. God sent His Son to win man back. In other words, God will not give up on you, so do not you give up on God. Paul wrote in 1 Timothy 1:15–16,

> Here is a trustworthy saying that
> deserves full acceptance: Christ Jesus came

into the world to save sinners—of whom I am the worst. But for that very reason I was shown mercy so that in me, the worst of sinners, Christ Jesus might display His unlimited patience as an example for those who would believe on Him and receive eternal life. (NIV)

Paul, one of the greatest writers of the New Testament, called himself the worst sinner in history. You see, he spent his life seeking out and killing anyone who followed Jesus. He was a Christian killer when Jesus called him. Paul writes, "I thank God for saving me through Jesus Christ our Lord." Paul further writes that the mercy shown him is an example of the saving grace of Jesus for those who believe on Him. So, yes, there is hope. There was hope for Paul, and there is hope for you and me. Jesus is our blessed hope. Jesus, and only Jesus, can give eternal life. Man cannot do anything alone for salvation.

In the February 2017 issue of *Our Daily Bread* devotional, David Roper wrote,

And here's the best part. It's a gift! All you have to do is receive the salvation Jesus offers. C. S. Lewis, musing on this notion, describes it as something like "a chuckle in the darkness"—the sense that something that simple is the answer. Some say, "It's too simple." Well, I say, if God loved you even before you were born and wants you to live with Him forever, why would He make it hard?

We expect something more complicated, but God's plan is simple. That is why so many people miss it. It is too good to be true.

CHAPTER 3

The Greatest Gift
(SALVATION CANNOT BE EARNED—IT'S A GIFT)

Romans 6:23 states, "For the wages of sin is death; but **the gift of God** is eternal life" (emphasis mine). Your sinful nature will always keep you out of heaven unless you accept the gift. You are not good enough or pure enough to get to heaven on your own. **You need the gift that God has given** to everyone who will accept it, **the gift of Jesus Christ.** The Bible says in John 3:16 (KJV), "For God so loved the world that **He gave His only begotten Son** [emphasis mine] that whosoever believed in Him would not perish but would have everlasting life."

God knows your frailties. He knows your humanity. He knows you cannot do it by yourself. That is why He sent His Son. The next verse says, "For God sent not His Son into the world to condemn the world, but that the world through Him might be saved" (John 3:17 KJV).

Jesus left His heavenly home in glory to come to this sin-sick world for one reason—to save us, to rescue me and you from Satan. First Timothy 2:4 tells us that God desires that all men be saved. Second Peter 3:9 (KJV) states, "He is not willing that any should perish." God loves us so much He wants us to live forever with Him in heaven.

That is why Jesus was born that day in Bethlehem for one purpose and one purpose alone—to die in our place. To pay the debt for our sins. The Bible in Matthew 20:28 says He gave His life "as a ransom for many." In Matthew 1:21, the angel of the Lord appeared to Joseph to assure him that Mary, who was pledged to be married to him, had not been unfaithful. He told Joseph, "She will give birth to a son, and you are to give Him the name Jesus because **He will save His people from their sins.**" Not only did the angel tell Joseph what to name the baby but also that **Jesus would save His people from their sin.** In the Bible, Luke 2:10–11 (KJV), an angel appeared to the shepherds:

> And the angel said unto them, Fear not: for, behold, I bring you good tidings of great joy, which shall be to all people. For unto you is born this day in the city of David a Saviour, which is Christ the Lord.

Notice the angel said good news for ALL THE PEOPLE. So why was Jesus born for "all the people"? **Because God loves all people, atheist as well as religious.** The Bible tells us in John 3:16 (KJV), "For God so loved the world that He gave His only begotten Son **that whosoever believed in Him** would not perish but would have everlasting life." WHOSOEVER BELIEVED means all the people who believe would be saved. Jesus was the Savior of the world, and **He gave His life for all who would accept Him.** Now that is love.

The prophet Isaiah foretold the story long ago of Jesus's birth when he prophesied in Isaiah 9:6 (KJV), "For unto us a child is born, unto us a Son is given: and the government shall be upon His shoulder: and His name shall be called Wonderful, Counsellor, the Mighty God, the Everlasting Father, the Prince of Peace." Did you noticed he said **a Son is** *given*? **God gave the greatest gift** of all to the world that Christmas Day two thousand years ago in the little town of Bethlehem. **God gave His Son** because He loved us so much, He wanted us to live in heaven forever with Him. **There is only one requirement—we must believe that God's Son was born, died, was buried, and was raised from the dead and now sits at the right hand of God the Father in heaven.** The Bible says in Romans 10:9 (KJV), "That if thou shalt confess with thou mouth the Lord Jesus, and shalt believe in thine heart that God hath raised Him from the dead, thou shalt be saved." That is called faith. In other words, you did not see it, but you believe it. **The key is you must believe.**

The disciple Thomas did not believe the others when they told him that Jesus had risen from the dead and that they had seen Him. Jesus later appeared to Thomas and told him to put his fingers into His pierced hands and side. Then Thomas believed. Jesus then said, "Blessed are those who have not seen, and yet have believed" (John 20:29). **Faith is believing. The Bible tells us "For we walk by faith, not by sight" (2 Cor. 5:7 KJV).** Sometimes, walking by faith defies all logic. Faith is not always rooted in what you understand. We must trust God when what He says does not make sense to us. The Bible tells us that His ways are not our ways, and His thoughts are not our thoughts. Sometimes when God is working in your life, you must ignore logic and walk by faith. He will never lead you wrong.

God wanted to make sure that we did not take credit for our salvation. He wanted to make sure that we could not brag about how much money we put in church, or how faithful we are, or perhaps how we are a good missionary. The Bible makes it plain in Ephesians 2:8–9 when it says, "For it is by grace you have been saved, through faith and not of yourself, it is **the *gift* of God**, not by works so that no one can boast." There is that word *gift* again. In other words, no man or woman is good enough to go to heaven without God's grace. (Grace is unmerited favor. It is when you get something you do not deserve.) Heaven knows none of us deserve **the *gift***, for the Bible says, "For we all have sinned and come short of the glory of God" (Rom. 3:23 KJV). That means me, you, the pope, the preacher, the deacon, missionary, and everybody else. None of us deserve to go to heaven. **But—thank God for Jesus—the *gift*.**

We all have a decision to make. Every person is going to spend eternity somewhere, and it is determined by whether we choose to accept or reject **God's *gift* of His Son Jesus as our Savior.**

If you want to be absolutely sure of your destination, then you need to **accept the *gift*.** For the Christian, death is the end of pain and suffering, not the end of life. *Miracle from Heaven* is a 2016 movie based on the true story of a young girl named Annabel Beam who had an incurable disease and lived a life of pain.

While playing in a tree in her backyard, she fell head-first into the hollow trunk of the tree. She hung there in so much pain she prayed to Jesus that she would die and go live with Him so she would be free from pain. The mother of this child had taught her to always trust that God had a better plan for her life, and this young girl was so sure of her destination she knew that if she died, she would go to heaven and be free from pain. During her tree experience, Jesus healed her, and when examined in the hospital, no evidence could be found of the disease. The Lord healed her that day because of her faith. Wouldn't you like that kind of blessed assurance, being so confident that you will go to heaven that you would even ask to die? Jesus said in John 11:25, "He who believes in me will live even though he dies." You should be that sure and that confident of your salvation. We should all have that certainty of our final destiny.

God gave us a gift that money cannot buy, yet it is the most precious gift ever given. Roman 6:23 (KJV) tells us, **"The *gift* of God is eternal life through Jesus Christ our Lord."** To accept Jesus as Savior is to **accept His gift of salvation offered on the cross. It is the perfect gift, but it is only good if we accept it. Accept the *gift* and live forever in heaven. It is the gift that keeps on giving.**

CHAPTER 4

Only One Way
(THANK GOD FOR JESUS)

Did you notice that the common denominator in all the salvation scriptures is **Jesus**? That is because He, Jesus, and **He, Jesus, alone is the only way to heaven. There is no other way.** In John 14:1–6 (KJV), Jesus is speaking: "Let not your hearts be troubled. Believe in God, believe also in Me (Jesus). For in My Father's house are many mansions. If it were not so I (Jesus) would have told you. I (Jesus) go to prepare a place for you, and if I (Jesus) go to prepare a place for you, I will come again to receive you unto Myself so that where I (Jesus) am, you will also be. Where I (Jesus) go, you know, and the way you know."

Philip answered, "Lord, we do not know where You are going, and neither do we know the way."

Jesus answered, "**I (Jesus)** AM THE WAY, the truth, and the life. No man comes to the Father but by Me (Jesus)."

Neither is there salvation in any other: for **there is none other name** under heaven given among men, whereby we must be saved. (Acts 4:12 KJV)

All the prophets testify about Him [Jesus] that everyone who believes in Him [Jesus] receives forgiveness of sins through His name [Jesus]. (Acts 10:43)

And they said, believe on the Lord Jesus Christ and thou shall be saved. (Acts 16:31 KJV)

And this is the record, that God hath given to us eternal life and this life is in His Son [Jesus]. He that hath the Son hath life; and He that hath not the Son of God hath not life. (1 John 5:11–12 KJV)

He that believe on the Son [Jesus] hath everlasting life and he that believe not the Son [Jesus] shall not see life, but the wrath of God abides on him. (John 3:36 KJV)

In John 6:28, the crowd asked Jesus what we must do to do the works God requires. Jesus answered, "The work of God is this. To believe in the One [Jesus] He has sent." Verse 38 goes on to say, "For I [Jesus] have come down from heaven not to do My will but to do the will of Him who sent Me." John 6:40 says, "For my Father's will is that everyone who looks to the Son [Jesus] and believes in Him [Jesus] shall have eternal life and I will raise him up at the last day."

All through the Bible is scripture telling us that we must believe in Jesus, God's Son, in order to go to heaven. **Believing in God the Father alone will not get us there. As scripture after scripture tells us, we must believe in God's son Jesus, for Jesus is the one and only way to heaven. There is no other way.**

We are safe in God's love from the moment we accept Jesus as our Savior until the moment God takes us home to glory. As stated in John 10:28, "I [Jesus] give them eternal life and they shall never perish." Even in the Old Testament, Isaiah writes, "I [Jesus], even I [Jesus], am the Lord and besides me [Jesus] there is no other Savior" (Isaiah 43:11 KJV).

The two most popular scriptures quoted regarding salvation are the same ones Rev. Townsend told Queen Victoria to read: John 3:16 (KJV), which says, "For God so loved the world that He gave His only begotten Son [Jesus] that whosoever believed in Him (Jesus) will not perish but will have everlasting life;" and Romans 10:9 (KJV): "If you confess with your mouth the Lord Jesus and believe in your heart that God raised Him (Jesus) from the dead thou shall be saved."

If you are sure of your salvation, you can say what the apostle Paul wrote in 2 Timothy 1:12 (KJV): "[F]or I know whom I have believed and am persuaded that He [Jesus] is able to keep what I have committed to Him [Jesus] until that day." **Scripture after scripture is written to help you to be sure of your salvation.**

> He who has the Son [Jesus] has life and he who does not have the Son of God [Jesus] does not have life. I write these things to you who believe in the name of the Son of God [Jesus] so that you may know that you have eternal life. (1 John 5:12–13)

We have two choices: either believe Jesus and go to heaven, or reject Jesus and go to hell. I once attended a church service where the preacher ended his message by saying that he would rather go through this life believing that there is a God and die and find out that there is not a God than to go through life not believing in God then die and find out that there is a God. For it will be too late then. To make it more relevant, I would rather go through life believing that Jesus is the only way to heaven, die, and find out there are also other ways, than to go through life believing there are other ways, die, and find out that Jesus is the only way. **Once you die, your destiny is sealed. There is no turning back, no second chance.**

In the Scriptures (Matt. 3:17, 17:5; Mark 9:7 KJV), God spoke three times acknowledging Jesus as His Son: "This is My beloved Son in whom I am well pleased." He had left His home in glory and walked this sin-sick world for thirty-three years, preaching, teaching, healing the sick, restoring sight to the blind, casting out demons, performing miracle after miracle, then offering up His life as a ransom for many. Romans 5:7–8 states,

> Very rarely will anyone die for a righteous man, though for a good man someone might possibly dare to die. But God demonstrates His own love for us in this: while we were still sinners, Christ died for us.

Now it does not get any more real than that. Now you tell me what Savior you know that is still alive and equal to that. There is none. And those manmade statues and gods that have been fashioned out of stone and marble cannot save you. They cannot even hear you. Those prophets and professed gods that have been showing up and making claims of a better life for you if you follow them—why have they just decided to come on the scene now? Watch out! The Bible tells us about false prophets. They are called wolves in sheep's clothing. Beware, my friend. They have come to steal and kill. Please do not fall prey to their lies and deceit. There is no other Savior. There is no other way. There is only one way—Jesus, and He lives!

The Bible was written over two thousand years ago, and the Bible dedicates more space to the subject of prophecy than almost any other subject. Biblical prophecy is still revealing truth as it unfolds today. Signs and signals of the end times as foretold centuries ago are coming to pass. There are many signs which have already come to pass, many we are experiencing now, and there are many more to come. The Bible has survived all these years because of God's great love for us and the fact that He wants all of us to live with Him in eternity. Because of His grace and His mercy, He provided a way through His Son Jesus. The foretelling of Jesus's birth, death, and resurrection was recorded in Scripture long before He was born. After His death on the cross for our sins and His resurrection from the dead, the Bible records that He was seen by more than five hundred people (1 Cor. 15:3–8).

In the Bible, the gospel of John describes how after Jesus had risen from the dead, He appeared to His disciples. The scripture tells us in John 20:24–31,

> Now Thomas (called Didymus) one of the twelve was not with the disciples when Jesus came. So the other disciples told him, "We have seen the Lord." But he said to them, "Unless I see the nail marks in His hands and put my finger where the nails were and put my hand into His side, I will not believe it." A week later His disciples were in the house again and Thomas was with them. Though the doors were locked, Jesus came and stood among them and said, "Peace be with you." Then He said to Thomas, "Put your fingers here, see my hands. Reach out your hand and put it into my side. Stop doubting and believe." Thomas said to Him, "My Lord and my God." Then Jesus told him, "Because you

have seen Me you have believed; blessed are those who have not seen and yet have believed. Jesus did many other miraculous signs in the presence of His disciples that are not recorded in this book." But these are written that you may believe that Jesus is the Christ, the Son of God, and that by believing, you may have life in His name.

Acts 1:3 states, "After His suffering He showed Himself to these men and gave many convincing proofs that He was alive. He appeared to them over a period of forty days and spoke about the kingdom of God."

The Bible tells us that forty days after His resurrection, Jesus ascended back to His Father, and today, Jesus still lives in heaven and is seated at the right hand of God, making intercessions for us. People will challenge you and differ from you on the fact that Jesus is the only way to heaven. One day you too will live in heaven with Him if you accept Him as your Savior and Lord. What about all the other religions? Will they not go to heaven? they will argue. In author Max Lucado's book *Grace for the Moment* (volume 1), the devotional reading for April 16 entitled "The Only Path," Lucado talks about tolerance and the ability to be understanding of those with whom you differ.

He stated that Jesus was tolerant of many things: His disciples when they doubted, the crowds that misunderstood, and us when we fall. There was one area, however, where Jesus was intolerant. He was adamant and utterly unyielding. When it comes to salvation, there are not several roads; there is only one road. There are not several paths; there is only one path. There are not several ways but only one way, Jesus Himself. "That is why it is so hard for people to believe in Jesus," Lucado writes. "It is much easier to consider Him one of several options rather than *the* option. But such a philosophy is no option."

There is no option. Jesus is the only way. Jesus said, "I am the Way, the Truth, and the Life. No man comes to the Father but by Me." So your answer should be, "Jesus said it, I believe it, and that settles it."

CHAPTER 5

Dead Man Walking
(Physically Alive, Spiritually Dead)

If you do not know Jesus, you are spiritually dead. Physically you may be alive and walking, but spiritually you are dead. All of us are born in sin because of the first man, Adam. And because of the first man, Adam, we are all doomed to die a sinner's death.

A Perfect World (Gen. 1:1–2:3)

When God created man and woman, **they were without sin, perfect in a perfect world**, the garden of Eden. The Bible tells us God created man for His good purpose. He gave man everything he needed for a perfect life. He gave him a wife for companionship, and He gave him food. The Bible tells us in Genesis 1:26–2:9 that God put man in charge of all the animals He created. God walked with man in the garden of Eden and fellowshipped with him. God loved man, and He wanted man to love Him of his own free will, so He gave man the ability to choose. Man did not have to work, just enjoy life and be a friend to God, and **man would live forever in this paradise garden**.

The garden was full of all kinds of trees, and the Lord God told Adam He was free to eat from any tree in the garden except from the tree of the knowledge of good and evil, which stood in the middle of the garden, for if he ate of it, he would surely die (Gen. 2:16–17). That was the only tree from which Adam and Eve were forbidden to eat. All the other trees were there for them to enjoy. Only one was off-limits to the pair. God instructed them that **if they ate from that tree, they would surely die**. In the Bible, the first book, Genesis, gives the full account of God's creation of earth and mankind and how sin entered the otherwise perfect world.

Sin Enters the World (Gen. 3:6)

Adam and Eve disobeyed God and ate the fruit from the forbidden tree. That was the first sin, and that sin of disobedience separated man from God. **From that day forward, man was no longer perfect and would always be born in sin.** God is holy and perfect and righteous and cannot tolerate sin. Since we all came from the first man, Adam, all mankind has Adam's DNA, and that DNA is sinful. In other words, Adam had tainted blood. The Bible tells us that everyone is made from one blood. Acts 17:26 (KJV) states, "And hath made of one blood all nations of men to dwell on the face of the earth and hath determined the times before appointed and the bounds of their habitation." **Since we are all born of Adam's sinful blood, we will all die because the price for sin is death.** God warned Adam that he would surely die if he ate of the forbidden tree. The Bible tells us that death entered the world through this one man (Adam), and through him, sin passed to all people (Rom. 5:12 and 1 Cor. 15:22).

The Penalty for Sin—Death (Rom. 6:23)

Before Adam sinned, the Bible tells us that Adam walked with God. He had fellowship with God in the garden of Eden. But not only did Adam's sin of disobedience separate him from God; since we are all born in sin because of Adam, we too are separated from God at birth. **We are now all born with a sin nature and a death sentence that has been handed down from generation to generation.** We are not only doomed to die a physical death but also doomed to live a spiritual death. We are dead men walking, physically alive but spiritually dead. You see, sin had separated us from God. We could no longer be in God's presence because He is a holy and righteous God, and we were dead in our sins and offensive to a perfect and just God. Not only is God a righteous God, He is also a just God. Since the wages of sin is death, and God had pronounced a death sentence on sin, someone had to pay the penalty for justice to be served.

Ransom Paid on the Cross (John 3:16)

Because of God's love for us and because of His mercy and His grace, God provided a way to make us right with Him again—He sent His Son, Jesus, to pay the price and bridge the gap between man and God. The Bible tells us how God's perfect Son, Jesus, bore the sins of the whole world when He died a horrific death on the cross and shed His blood for you and me. **Christ's death on the cross redeemed us. Redemption means payment of a ransom.** It was His blood that covered our sins so that we could be made right with God. As the old hymn goes, "What can wash away my sins? Nothing but the blood of Jesus." Through His suffering, Jesus paid the price for the sins of the whole world. Jesus died in our place. The Bible tells us that He died, was buried, and on the third day, He rose from the dead and now sits in heaven at the right hand of God the Father, making intercessions for us. He died so that we might live forever with Him. The Bible tells us that "God so loved the World that He gave His only begotten Son that whosoever believed in Him should not perish but have eternal life" (John 3:16 KJV). Jesus is our Savior. He is the only one who can save us from our sins and make us whole and spiritually alive. But there is only one condition. The Bible says, "**Whosoever believes in Him** shall have everlasting life." **We must believe in Jesus**.

Repent: Be Born Again (John 3:3)

All He asks is that you confess that you are a sinner in need of a Savior and believe that Jesus died, was buried, and rose again. **Repent and live for Him. It is as simple as that. The moment you accept Jesus as Lord of your life, you are born again**, and you become a new creation. This is called the new birth. Second Corinthians 5:17 says, "Therefore, if anyone is in Christ, he is a new creation. The old things have passed away; behold the new has come." This means that anyone who belongs to Christ has become a new person. The old life is gone; a new life has begun. You are no longer what you used to be and will never revert to that old condition. You have been reborn.

In John 3:3 (KJV), when Nicodemus asked Jesus how he could be saved, Jesus told him, "Except a man be born again he cannot see the kingdom of God." Notice the word *again*. Nicodemus asked, "How can a man be born when he is old? Surely he cannot enter a second time into his mother's womb to be born." Jesus explained that the **first birth is a fleshly birth** born in the flesh of your mother's womb, with Adam's DNA. Since Adam, all mankind has been born with tainted blood, blood tainted by the sin of Adam. **Only the blood of Jesus (the perfect man) can wash away that sin and make us spiritually alive.** The **second birth is a spiritual birth**, born of the Spirit of God. This spiritual birth happens the moment you accept Jesus as your Lord and Savior. The Holy Spirit comes and lives in you forever, allowing you to be saved from your sins and to go to heaven.

First Corinthians 15:49 tells us that just as we are born in the likeness of the earthly man (Adam), so shall we bear the likeness of the man from heaven (Jesus) in our spiritual birth. Until we are born again by the Holy Spirit, our nature remains unchanged. **But when we are born again, we become children of God. John 1:12–13 states,**

**Yet to all who received Him to those
who believed on His name He gave the**

right to become children of God, children born not of natural descent nor of human decision, or a husband's will, but born of God.

Galatians 3:26 (KJV) tells us, "For ye are all the children of God by faith in Christ Jesus."

You may not feel any different, or hear bells ringing or fireworks going off. You may not feel faint or have some out-of-body experience, but you will begin to feel God working in your life. In fact, do not expect your life to now become all peaches and cream, all fuzzy and warm with no problems or conflicts. Quite the contrary. It will not always be easy to live your new life as a Christian, a child of God. The moment the Lord becomes the center of your life, Satan will start bombarding you with all kinds of problems. You see, you no longer belong to him, and he does not like that. You will still struggle with temptation and sin. The world will try to remind you of all the things you used to do. But once you are born again, you have the Holy Spirit living in you to help you overcome the temptations of the world.

The New Birth; the Holy Spirit (John 14:26, Acts 2:38)

You see, God had a plan, a plan that would not only save us but also restore us to a right relationship with Him. And that plan was Jesus. You are no longer a dead man walking. **You are made spiritually alive by the Holy Spirit** who comes to indwell you with your new birth. It is the Holy Spirit within that enables us to live the Christian life. When we surrender our lives to Christ, He gives us His Holy Spirit, who empowers us to choose between right and wrong. God's indwelling Spirit empowers you to want to live for Him. You have a new identity, and with it should come a new attitude. You are physically and spiritually alive in Christ, a child of God and heir to the kingdom of heaven, which all happened at the moment of salvation.

One new believer described it as something strange happening, a curious discomfort. Once saved, I could not relax with myself. What happened to me? I had been exposed to Jesus. Before Jesus, my life was a mess, and I did not even know I was a mess until I met Jesus. Now I was no longer comfortable with the dirty jokes or off-color remarks. I had become a new creature because old things had passed away. They were gone. My behavior began to showcase the change made in my life by following Jesus. I began to face uncertainty with peace. I was no longer a dead man walking. I was now alive in Christ. Ephesians 2:4 (emphasis mine) states, "Because of His great love for us, **God who is rich in mercy made us alive with Christ** even when we were dead in transgression—it is by grace you have been saved."

CHAPTER 6

Faith

(CAN'T SEE HIM, BUT YOU KNOW HE'S THERE)

In the Bible, Hebrews 11:1 tells us that "faith is being sure of what we hope for and certain of what we do not see." We all are saved in the same way, **by faith alone** (Rom. 3:24–30), and we all become the children of God **through faith in Christ Jesus** (Gal. 3:26). **Through faith in Jesus, we receive God's pardon and escape sin's penalty.** The Bible tells us that **"without faith it is impossible to please God** because anyone who comes to Him must believe that He exists and that He rewards those who earnestly **seek Him"** (Heb. 11:6). He wants you to seek Him. God actually **rewards those who earnestly seek Him.** Are you earnestly **seeking Him?** Do you want to know Him for yourself?

God says in Jeremiah 29:13, "You will **seek Me** and find Me when you **seek Me** with all your heart." In other words, *If you look hard enough, you will find Me.*

Deuteronomy 4:29 says, "But if you **seek the Lord your God** you will find Him if you look for Him with all your heart and soul." Now He is saying to put your soul in it too. With all your heart and soul means with your very core. With everything you got. Are you genuinely **seeking Him?** Talk to Him, tell Him you want to know Him, and ask Him to come into your heart. God wants you to **seek Him**; He wants you to know Him.

Acts 17:22–31 states that God has made humanity in the earth so that they may **seek Him.** Man is born with a void in his life—a deep yearning, a missing piece due to Adam's sin. That missing piece is God. Romans 4:19 states, "For just as through the disobedience of one man [Adam] the many were made sinners so through the obedience of the one man [Jesus] the many will be made righteous." Although Adam's sin separated man from God, God provided a way to make man right with Him (i.e., righteous) again through His Son, Jesus. He can restore your relationship with God, the missing piece in your life. He loves you and is just waiting for you to want to know Him, to **seek Him. Are you a sincere seeker? Or are you too busy? If you slow down and take time to look around, you will find Him. He is waiting for you.**

Jesus said in John 6:38–40,

For I have come down from heaven
not to do my will but to do the will of
Him who sent me. And this is the will of
Him who sent me that I shall lose none
of all that He has given me but raise them
up at the last day. For my Father's will is
that everyone who looks to the Son and
believes in Him shall have eternal life and
I will raise him up at the last day.

Jesus wants you to know how wide and long and high
and deep His love for you is so that you will know His love
that surpasses all knowledge (Eph. 3:18–19). He would
rather die than live without you. Now that is love. He loves
you enough to die for you, a sinner. Like the songwriter
wrote, "I don't know why Jesus loves me; I don't know why
He cares. I don't know why He sacrificed His life, but, oh,
I'm so glad He did." He gave His life, died on the cross
so that we might live eternally with Him in heaven. He
paid our sin debt and restored our relationship with God
the Father. All that He asks of us is to admit that we are
sinners, ask for forgiveness, and believe that His Son Jesus
Christ died to pay for our sins. Acknowledging Jesus as
Lord, admitting your sins, and asking for forgiveness, you
can have friendship with God through Christ. You will

have all the privileges of His divine protection, such as the following:

1) *Being your constant companion.* For in His Word, He promises never to leave you or forsake you.

2) *Access to Him in prayer.* He is always listening. No busy signals.

3) *Being your advocate.* He sits at the right hand of God, making intercessions for you.

4) *Forgiveness of your sins* when you go to Him with a contrite heart and will remember them no more.

5) *Peace*, that supernatural calm that comes only from having a relationship with Jesus. Scripture tells us in Isaiah 26:3 (KJV), "Thou wilt keep him in perfect peace, whose mind is stayed on thee: because he trusteth in thee."

The moment you accept Jesus Christ as your Savior, the Holy Spirit comes and lives in you. He will direct you in all things. **God is faithful and keeps His Word, but He expects you to do your part by loving and obeying Him. You do not need to be perfect, but you need to be faithful.**

The Bible tells us of people who went to great lengths to **seek Jesus**. In the third chapter of John, Nicodemus, a

Pharisee and religious leader of his day, climbed a tree to see Jesus. Mark 2:4 tells of how friends of a paralyzed man, when they could not get through the crowd, took parts of the roof off a house to let their friend down in the crowd in front of Jesus. In the nineteenth chapter of Matthew, the rich man asked Jesus how to get into His kingdom. Jesus's life started with wise men **seeking Him** and shepherds traveling from afar to worship Him as a baby in a manger (see Matthew 2). And even today, wise men still **seek Him.** Are you **seeking Him?** If you are wise, you too will **seek Him** while He can still be found. **Seek God** in good times, **seek Him** in bad times, and you will always find Him watching over you. Our heavenly Father knows what you need even before you ask. Matthew 6:33 states, "But **seek first the kingdom of God and His righteousness** and all these things will be given to you as well." **Seek Him**, and everything else will fall into place. You will find that the more you get to know Him, the more you want to know. It is like tasting something and finding out it is so good you want more, and the more you eat the more you want. You cannot get enough. This same analogy is used in Scripture concerning God. The Bible says in Psalm 34:8 (KJV), "Oh taste and see that the Lord is good."

As you **seek Him**, your faith will grow. Spiritual growth should be a continual process throughout your life. As your faith and relationship with the Lord develops, you will notice Him moving in your life.

You will begin to see things differently. Old habits will no longer have a hold on you. Things that you used to accept will begin to bother you. Certain words will offend you. Worldly things will lose their appeal to you. Why? Because as you **seek God**, He opens your eyes and reveals the negative things of the world. Evil will be more apparent to you, and you will no longer accept its hold on you.

You will feel uncomfortable with sin and will reach out to God for forgiveness and change. This transformation is gradual, and it does not happen overnight. The more you **seek God**, the more you will feel His presence in your life. The Bible says, "Come near to God and He will come near to you" (James 4:8). He is like Scotch tape; you cannot see Him, but you know He is there. You will begin to walk by faith, not by sight (2 Cor. 5:7 KJV). As you start living close to God, you will feel a peace and a calm that cannot be explained.

Having a personal experience with Jesus is life-changing. Your character and conversation will change as you begin to live out your faith. Good works and faithful service will become evidence of the Holy Spirit working in you.

Your life will begin to reflect an unspeakable joy that had been missing. Each day, you will begin to know His blessed hope as you recognize Him moving in your life. You will become aware as you awaken to His love all around you and His mercy and grace following you.

You will begin to call "luck" for what it is—not "luck" but "blessings," realizing that "every good and perfect gift is from above" (James 1:17 KJV). You will begin to want to please Jesus as His Holy Spirit works in your life.

You will have a new attitude as Scripture describes in Ephesians 4:22–24 (NIV),

> You were taught, with regards to your former way of life, to put off your old self, which is being corrupted by its deceitful desires, to be made new in the attitude of your minds, and to put on the new self, created to be like God in true righteousness and holiness.

Philippians 2:5 says, "Your attitude should be the same as that of Christ Jesus" (NIV). This is saying that Jesus should be our prime example. You are probably familiar with the song the children sing, "WWJD: What Would

Jesus Do?" Can you imagine what this world would be like if every Christian asked themselves what Jesus would do?

You can start today by asking Jesus to come into your heart. Someone told me about Jesus and changed my life. Jesus is a lifesaver. Not only did He change my life, but He also saved it. He will do the same for you. He is just waiting for you to ask Him to be your Savior. Admit that you are a sinner and cannot save yourself. That you believe Jesus is the Son of God who died on the cross for your sins and that you want to turn your life around and live for Him. **If you truly accept the Lord Jesus as your personal Savior, you can be assured that you are going to heaven. That sincere prayer of faith will make you a part of God's family and heir to His kingdom. Someone described faith as a feeling of security at all times. It's a great feeling.**

If you have not already found a place to worship, ask God to help you find a church where you can fellowship with other believers. Become a participating member. Do not just show up and keep the pews warm. Getting involved is necessary for your spiritual growth. You have just made the best decision that you will ever make in your entire lifetime—the decision to live for Jesus. Welcome to God's family. Your destination is now guaranteed, but your journey has just begun.

CHAPTER 7

Destination Guaranteed
(ONCE SAVED, ALWAYS SAVED)

You cannot lose your salvation. John 11:25 states, "He who believes in Me will live even though he dies." For the Christian, death is the end of pain and suffering but not the end of life. We will live forever in heaven. When this old body dies, we pass from this life to the next life. **Heaven is guaranteed for the Christian.**

Jesus is like Colonial Penn Life Insurance—

1) *Will take you just as you are.* Jesus said, "I have not come to call the righteous, but sinners" (Mark 2:17).

2) *You are locked in for life.* Ephesians 4:30 (KJV) tells us "we are sealed until the day of redemption."

3) *Acceptance is guaranteed.* "[H]aving believed you are sealed with the Holy Spirit of promise who

is the guarantee of our inheritance until the day of redemption," says Ephesians 1:14, and "He anointed us, set his seal of ownership on us, and put His Spirit in our hearts as a deposit, guaranteeing what is to come" (2 Cor. 1:22, 5:5).

Once you accept Christ, the devil gets really busy in your life. **Satan does not want you to belong to God; he wants you to belong to him.** Remember, we live in a fallen world, and sin is everywhere. Satan is real, and he will come at you in all kinds of disguises and distractions. He will come at you through your family, your friends, and anyone else that he thinks is close to you. The first thing he attacks is your mind. **Recognize your enemy. Your enemy is the devil. All evil comes from the devil.** Be warned, my friend, for the Bible says the devil roams the earth seeking whom he can destroy. The Bible calls him the "prince of this world," and all things evil belong to him, including evil people. Be careful of the devil's ploy and schemes. He knows our weakness and how to exploit them. He wants you to feel like you have not been saved. If you stumble, do not assume that you are not truly saved. If you have the old desires, do not assume you have not been born again. If your mind wanders when trying to pray, do not be alarmed. It happens sometimes to all of us. If you make a mistake, it only means that you are human. **Your mistakes will not stop God from loving you. Your behavior, whether good or bad, will never affect God's unconditional love for you.**

Even when you accept Christ and are born again into God's family, you will still have the old sin nature. We have a God who loves us in spite of our failures. We are all deeply flawed. We all have struggles with guilt. Even the apostle Paul said that when he wants to do good, evil is always present. The apostle Paul wrote in Romans 7:18, "I know that nothing good lives in me, that is, in my sinful nature. For I have the desire to do what is good, but I cannot carry it out." He goes on further in verse 21: "When I want to do good, evil is always present." **This is the internal spiritual battle that wages war in all of us.** It is how we all struggle with sin. In Galatians 5:17, Paul further describes the struggle between our spiritual nature and our sinful nature:

> For the sinful nature desires what is
> contrary to the Spirit, and the Spirit what
> is contrary to the sinful nature. They are
> in conflict with each other so that you do
> not do what you want.

So do not lose heart when you find yourself doubting your salvation. That is Satan trying to make you doubt if you are saved. **Remember that once saved, always saved. You cannot lose your salvation.**

You have heard people often characterize one sin as worse than the other, a big sin or a little sin. There is no such thing. Sin is sin, and being spiritually separated from God is the real sin. **Jesus taught that God would forgive the worst sinner. If you do not have a personal relationship with God, you are living in sin, no matter what you do or do not do**. A lot of people confuse religion with relationship, but religion without relationship is worthless. Religion is an outward expression of spirituality but does not necessarily mean an inner conviction of the heart. Trusting Jesus changes the heart. **And you can only get this relationship through Jesus because only Jesus can reconcile you to God—make you right with God.**

Mart DeHaan, founder of the Radio Bible Class and coeditor of monthly devotional guide *Our Daily Bread* wrote in one of the *Discovery Series* booklets concerning the topic "Following Jesus (Relationship or Religion)," "Even those who call themselves Christians can be more focused on the routines or rituals of religion than on what they should be focused on—Jesus Christ." He further wrote, "Religion is what we do for God on the outside. Christ is what God does for us to change us from the inside." And oh, what a privilege it is to know Him personally. **Once you have that personal relationship, you have the trust, that blessed assurance that Jesus loves you no matter what.** That is why Whitney Houston, despite her struggles in life, which we all have in some form or fashion, could say with such confidence that she knew Jesus loved her.

The Bible says when you are dead to sin, you are alive in Christ because of the grace of God. It is only by God's grace. Which basically says you certainly do not deserve it. The Bible says, "What shall we say then? Shall we go on sinning so that grace can increase? By no means!" God's grace does not give us a license to sin. **What it does for the believer is give us a means by which we can always go to God and ask for forgiveness. It is because of our relationship with God through Jesus.** Anyone who allows sin to rule in his life is miserable and helpless. The conflict between flesh and spirit continues in us as long as we live. It is a spiritual struggle, and some people struggle more than others. But when we struggle against our sinful ways, grieve over them, and ask for forgiveness, God will hear our prayers and answer. God knows we are flawed, imperfect people. We need to understand that though we are imperfect people, we serve a perfect God. One who looks beyond our faults and sees our need. God loves us in spite of us.

The Bible says we all have sinned and come short of the glory of God (Rom. 6:23). Jesus is our Savior and the only one who can rescue us from sin.

The Christian knows that he is flesh as well as spirit and that he is indwelled by two forces that struggle against each other. The Christian knows that when he sins, he can go to God and ask for forgiveness. And once he receives God's forgiveness, he starts all over again. **What a privilege it is to belong to God's family and to know beyond a shadow of a doubt that your destination is guaranteed.** The Bible says in Romans 5:8, "While we were still sinners Christ died for us." Since Christ died for us, the ones who believe in Him are not condemned. Many times in our faith walk, we take the wrong path; we ignore the prompting of the Holy Spirit and go our own way. But once we realize our mistake, a believer turns around and goes the other way. He repents, and the power of the Spirit identifies him as being in Christ, and he is forgiven. No matter how much we struggle and suffer through the sin and shame of this life, God delivers the Christian. **No matter how terrible or how far we fall, if we truly belong to Christ, He picks us up. He does not leave us down, defeated, and discouraged but continues His work of forgiveness and grace in our lives.** As the popular song by Donnie McClurkin "We Fall Down" goes, "For a saint is just a sinner who fell down and got up." Throughout her struggles with the demons and strongholds in her life, Whitney Houston never lost consciousness of the fact that Jesus loved her. She fell down, but she would get up. She held on to her hope in Jesus. And that is what you need to do. Remember, Jesus loves you no matter what you have done or will do. It is called unconditional love.

Once you accept Christ, the Spirit of God comes and lives in you. The more you get to know Jesus, the more convinced you become of His love for you. You will begin to feel and see Him working in your life. The Bible says, "God began doing a good work in you and He will continue until it is finished when Jesus Christ comes again" (Phil. 1:6). It is a continuous process, like a newborn baby that has to crawl before he walks. He will get up and fall down many times before he masters walking. He will drink milk before he is able to eat solid food. It is a growing process, and so it is with a new Christian.

Remember, Christians are not perfect, just forgiven, and we will sin, but we do not live in sin. The Bible says, "If we claim to be without sin, we deceive ourselves and the truth is not in us" (1 John 1:8). The advantage of being a child of God is stated in the next verse: "If we confess our sins, He is faithful and just and will forgive us our sins and cleanse us from all unrighteousness." So do not lose heart.

The Christian can always go to God for forgiveness, and the Bible says He will not only forgive us our sins, He will remember it no more. Unlike friends and family who will keep a tally and will "forgive but not forget," God forgives and forgets, never to bring it up again. The Bible says no one can snatch you from His hands. John 10:28 says, "I give them eternal life and they shall never perish; no one can snatch them out of my hand."

You are always safe and secure in Jesus for the Bible says there is no condemnation for those who are in Christ Jesus (Rom. 8:1). The Christian is safe. Christ is around him, the Spirit is in him, and God is for him. The eighth chapter of Romans ends with the fact that **nothing can separate the Christian from the love of God.** Starting with verse 35, it reads,

> Who shall separate us from the love of Christ? Shall tribulation or distress, or persecution, or famine, or nakedness, or peril, or sword? As it is written, for thy sake we are killed all the day long; we are counted as sheep for the slaughter. Nay, in all these things we are more than conquerors through Him that loved us. For I am persuaded that neither death, nor life, nor

angels, nor principalities, nor powers, nor
things present, nor things to come, nor
height, nor depth, nor any other creature
shall be able to separate us from the love
of God which is in Christ Jesus our Lord.
(KJV)

We are now free from the guilt and penalty of sin and
are safe in the arms of Jesus.

Jesus will be with you wherever you go. He said in
Mathew 28:20 (KJV), "Lo, I am with you always even to
the end of the world." He promises in Hebrew 13:5 to
never leave you or forsake you. What a privilege to belong
to Him. You can go to Him for anything. I do not care how
bleak the situation looks or how there seems to be no way
out, you can trust God to be there for you. Remember, He
is God, and He can do anything. He can do the impossible.
God can make a way out of no way. Someone once wrote,
"You never know that God is all you need until God is
all you got." It is a good feeling to know for sure that you
belong to Him and that He has your back. No matter what
lies in our past, God forgives us when we confess our sins
and gives us a fresh start. **What a comfort it is to have that
blessed assurance, that guarantee of once saved, always
saved.**

CHAPTER 8

What's Next?
(MY NEW LIFE AS A CHRISTIAN)

Now that you know how easy it is to become a Christian, you can see that it is not complicated at all. You are now forever saved and safe in the arms of Jesus. However, the hard part is just beginning.

Living righteously is not easy, but the reward is great. Jesus tells us, "You must take up your cross and follow me" (Matt. 16:24; Mark 8:34; Luke 9:23). This means dying to self and living for Jesus. When you have accepted Jesus Christ as Lord and Savior of your life, you are saying, "NO" TO THE WORLD and "YES" TO CHRIST. You are now a new creature, *IN* THE WORLD BUT NOT *OF* THE WORLD. Christians are called to a higher standard than the world. This world is no longer your home; you are just passing through. You are now a citizen of God's kingdom, and you can now be assured that you are going to heaven.

The Bible tells us in Romans 12:2, "Do not conform any longer to the pattern of this world, but be transformed by the renewing of your mind." The Bible further says we are a peculiar people, chosen and set apart to do good works which God prepared in advance for us to do. Does this mean we will be free from trials and hardships? No. Jesus tells us in John 16:33 that "in this world you will have trouble, but take heart I have overcome the world." The Bible tells us that it rains on the just and the unjust. Matthew 5:45 says, "He causes His sun to rise on the evil and the good and sends rain on the righteous and the unrighteous." There will still be storms in your life, but Jesus will be there to take you through the storms. **He will provide a way when there seems to be no way out. You now have the Holy Spirit working in you to help guide you and show you the way.**

To be transformed by the renewing of your mind means you must fill your mind with scriptural truths so that you may grow in your knowledge of who God is. I cannot stress enough the importance of the Holy Bible for the Christian. It is God's love letter to us. It is our most valuable possession because it is God's revelation of Himself and His instructions to use. It is God's Word and your road map to life as a Christian. As a member of God's family, you need to get to know Him. His Word is truth and full of promises. Make it your goal to get to know Him better each day. Get a real Bible. There is nothing wrong with technology, but there is nothing like holding God's Holy Word in your hand and close to your heart. It will become your lifeline to Jesus. Get to know Him. The more you get to know Jesus, the more you will love Him. Learn His characteristics—He is love, He is peace, He is joy, He is hope, He is compassion, He is long-suffering, He is kind, He is patient, He is wise, He is gentle, He is all-powerful, He is all-present, He is faithful, He is everlasting, He is merciful, and His promises are true. He is the best friend you will ever have. **Let Him be your BFF.**

When you love someone, you want to know all about them. You want to spend time with them so you can get to know them better, you want to please them, you want to have a personal relationship with them. And so it is with Jesus. You should want to have a personal relationship, and each day as you work toward developing that relationship, it will get stronger and stronger. Our desire becomes to please Him in all we say and do and to love Him more and more. That is how you grow in Christ. As you begin the process of being spiritually transformed, you will experience a peace like you have never known. You will trust Him more each day as you begin to see Him working in your life. You will understand the true meaning of "No God, No Peace—Know God, Know Peace."

No truer words have been written. You will find that as you yield to the Holy Spirit's control and guidance in your life, He will help and equip you to live out your faith. Once you establish a relationship with Jesus, you will discover your life's purpose—He will reveal it to you.

It is so important that you study and know what you believe and why so that you can stand firm in your faith, not being swayed by every wind of new teaching and by the cunning and craftiness of people trying to trick you with lies so clever they sound like truth. On September 1, 2016, a documentary on CNN called *Holy Hell* told of a twenty-two-year search for the truth by a man who grew up with no guidance and who felt lost and empty like something was missing. He told of meeting a man who professed to be a teacher and promised to liberate the people. This man spoke four or five languages and had sessions called "cleansing." He was going to teach them how to see, hear, and taste God. They all lived together, played together, and ate together with other members and were separated from their families. They were told they had to be ready for God and would have to give up everything. They had no TV, no radio, no books, and had to ask for permission to communicate with family. The man being interviewed on CNN went on to say that this leader made him feel special and really loved. He said, "I would have killed or died for him."

As it turned out, it was, of course, a cult. That is why you need to know what you believe and why you believe it so you will not become a prime target for cults that add just enough truth to make their message believable. You must read, meditate, and study the Word of God, asking the Holy Spirit to help you understand. He will reveal to you the truth about Jesus so no one can deceive you by fine-sounding arguments. Colossians 2:8 states, "See to it that no one takes you captive through hollow and deceptive philosophy which depends on human tradition and the basic principles of this world rather than on Christ."

Sometimes when we are searching, we grab hold of anything that gives us instant gratification or happiness. We must, however, be diligent in our search for the truth. **Everything that looks good or feels good is not good.** In your search, be careful not to fall prey to the many false gods the Bible warns us about. Not everything you read, see, or hear on TV, radio, and the Internet is gospel. Anybody can be on Facebook and all the other social media available today. Beware! Just as social media can be used to spread God's message, the devil can also design and use all forms of disguises to prey on those who are weak and uninformed. That is why spiritual growth is so important. The Bible says in 2 Peter 3:17–18,

> Therefore, dear friends, since you already know this be on your guard so that you may not be carried away by the error of lawless men and fall from your secure position. But grow in the grace and knowledge of our Lord and Savior Jesus Christ. To Him be glory both now and forever more.

With your new life as a Christian, you can now face tomorrow with perfect peace, the peace and freedom that comes from knowing Jesus.

Now that you know Jesus, you need to share the good news. When anything good happens to us, we just cannot keep it to ourselves. Jesus is the best thing that will ever happen to you, so go shout it to the world. Tell your family, tell your friends, tell the world that you have accepted Jesus as your Lord and how He has given you the joy and peace you had been missing. Tell them your story of how you met Him when you were at your lowest point, and how He has changed your life. There are many people right now just like you were: lonely, lost, and sad, not knowing where to turn, not realizing what is missing in their lives. God has called me and you to tell a dying world of a living Savior named Jesus who is waiting and longing for them to seek Him. As Christians, we are called to be witnesses for Christ.

When the Holy Spirit came upon the disciples on the day of Pentecost, Peter stood up and preached before the crowd. We are also empowered by the Holy Spirit to be witnesses for Christ. The Holy Spirit will help you share the good news with others. You do not have to preach like Peter to get the message out to others; just share your story in conversation among friends and family. Not everyone will want to talk to you, but some will. Pray and ask the Holy Spirit to show you and guide you as you share what Jesus is doing in your life. Ask God to open their hearts as you share your faith with them.

Just remember to walk the talk. Let the things you say and do reveal the change in your life and reflect who you are now in Christ. As you grow in your faith, you will want those you love to experience the joy and peace you have from knowing Jesus. They will begin to see the change in you and will want to have that blessed assurance of an eternity with God.

CHAPTER 9

The Christian's Handbook
(THE BIBLE)

The Bible is God's written Word, His road map for His creation to help them navigate a fallen world and help them know what is of God and what is not of God. It is to show how His creation must be born again to become new creatures in order to live in the new world He is going to establish in His kingdom. The Bible tells of a new heaven and a new earth (Rev. 21:1), where all of God's creation will one day live in harmony. It tells of how He will one day return and gather all His creation, and will separate them for their final destination to be judged by the very one who was rejected by many (Jesus). The Bible tells how one day, Jesus will rule as King of kings and Lord of lords, and there will be, at last, peace on earth. That is our blessed hope. The Bible says that one day, every knee shall bow, and every tongue will confess that Jesus Christ is Lord (Phil. 2:10–

11). That is everyone, even those who rejected Jesus, will one day bow and acknowledge Him as Lord with fear and great trembling. Of course, it will be too late for them for they had already chosen their destination.

The Bible was written over two thousand years ago by approximately forty men chosen by God and divinely inspired by the Holy Spirit. It is the most popular book in all of history and has been the best-selling book in the world for years, although one survey indicated that only 12 percent of the people who said they believe the Bible read it every day. Practically every household owns at least one Bible, but it sits on the table collecting dust.

When I first visited my husband's childhood church, the old pastor stood at the pulpit with his Bible held high and told the congregation to hold their Bibles high so he could see them. If he saw that one did not have a Bible, he would call that person out by name and say, "Next Sunday, be sure to bring your Bible." I laughed after church about how ridiculous that was, and it was only until late in my Christian walk that I understood and truly appreciated that old preacher. Too bad today, we do not have more preachers like the late Pastor E. M. Elmore.

When I sit in church today as the Scripture is read, it is shown on a large screen, or people look at their cell phones or iPad. The irony is that when you sit behind people, you can see a lot of them texting or searching the Internet, or playing games on their gadgets, not looking at the scripture. Sadly, church used to be the only time they opened a Bible. Now they do not even open a Bible in church.

I learned to really appreciate the Bible and scripture reading when I started teaching the children's new members class. The first scripture we learned was Psalm 119:11: "I have hidden Your Word in my heart that I might not sin against You." It was important that they not only learn the scripture but also what it meant. I explained that when you already know the words to a song, you can say that you know that song by heart, meaning that you have memorized it. So when you hide God's Word in your heart, it means you have memorized it. Why? The scripture further says, "so I might not sin against You."

Now when you try to sin against God, His Holy Spirit, who lives in you, reminds you of what you have learned. The Holy Spirit cannot bring to your remembrance something that you never learned in the first place; you must know it. Ephesians 6:11 tells us to "put on the full armor of God so that you can take your stand against the devil's schemes." Part of that armor in verse 17 is the "sword of the Spirit, which is the Word of God." In the Bible, after Jesus was baptized, the devil tried three times to tempt Him, and each time, Jesus quoted scripture. Now if Jesus quoted scripture to rebuke the devil, should not we do the same?

In my class each week, the kids learned a new Bible verse that I printed on a three-by-five-inch card for them to take home. They were told to look at it during the day and at night before bedtime to read it and put it under their pillow, then repeat it over again during the week as they went to sleep. There is something very calming about repeating the words of Scripture aloud. The kids made Bible verse holders out of a clothespin and magnet to hold the card on the refrigerator door as a reminder to them. The kids were excited when it was time for them to recite the Bible verse and get a star on their chart. Once you learn it, you have it forever, and you can quote it, share it, or repeat it at night when your mind is on overdrive thinking about tomorrow and will not rest. Not only was my class learning these verses, but I was too. Now my repertoire of Scripture is extensive and a blessing in my life for me and for helping others. Yes, I am a Bible-toting, scripture-quoting Christian and proud of it. Jesus said, "If you are ashamed of Me, I will be ashamed of you before My Father."

I cannot emphasize enough the importance of your Bible. Diligently studying Scripture will help you discover who God is, what God means, and how He wants you to live. It will help you grow spiritually and increase your faith.

- Ask the Holy Spirit to direct you to join and be baptized in a good Bible-based church where Jesus is exalted and an uncompromising gospel is preached, taught, and practiced.

- Join a good Bible study group. This is so important for a new believer because some people teach only what itching ears want to hear. So you must search for sound doctrine regarding Jesus Christ crucified, buried, and resurrected.

- Purchase a good study Bible or reference Bible. All Bibles are not equal. The Bible was originally written in Hebrew and Greek, so sometimes the meaning is lost in translation. The King James Version remains the most popular, but the Old English text makes it difficult to understand. Most Bible scholars agree the New American Standard Bible is the most accurate English Bible translation, but there are others such as the New King James Version (NKJV) or the New International Version (NIV), which I have used in the writing of this book.

- You must discipline yourself to spend time alone with Jesus. Each time you open His Word, you are hearing God speaking to you directly. Take advantage of this privilege and read your Bible regularly. The most important time of your day is reading and meditating on the Word of God. Start your day with Jesus, praying, meditating, reading your Bible, and memorizing scripture. Never leave home in the morning without spending time in God's Word, if only for five minutes.

• Learn to practice His presence. No matter where you are, whether standing in line at the bank or grocery store, when you are sitting in traffic at a stop light, or when you are waiting in a doctor's office; use these times to make it a habit to think and meditate on Jesus. Remember, He is always with you no matter where you go. You never have to be lonely; you never have to be afraid. In Matthew 28, the last words spoken by Jesus before He ascended into heaven was, "Lo, I am with you always, even unto the end of the world." That, my friend, is forever. That is His promise, and His promises are true. He will never leave you or forsake you no matter what.

Jesus said heaven and earth will pass away, but His Word will never pass away (Matt. 24:35).

The Bible is God's love letter to us. Its message permeates with God's love from creation to the crucifixion and clearly reveals the way to Him through Jesus

Christ. The Bible is just as relevant today as it was centuries ago. One of our greatest needs today is for man to come back to the Scriptures as the basis of authority and to **read and study God's Word.** Yale University Professor, literary scholar, author, and preacher Dr. William Lyon Phelps stated, "I thoroughly believe in a university education for both men and women, but I believe a knowledge of the Bible without a college course is more valuable than a college course without the Bible."

BIBLIOGRAPHY

Chapter 1

Scriptures

Ecclesiastes 7:2

Hebrews 9:27

Romans 5:12

1 Corinthians 15:22

Romans 6:23

Matthew 7:21

John 3:16

Romans 10:9–10

Romans 8:1

John 4:18

Ecclesiastes 12:13–14

Ecclesiastes 3:11

Romans 8:38

References

Steve Jobs talks about death at the 2005 Stanford Commencement Address, accessible on YouTube (https://youtu.be/Hd_ptbiPoXM).

Albom, Mitch. *Tuesdays with Morrie.* Doubleday, 1997.

Barbara Walters's TV special, *Heaven: Where Is It? How Do We Get There?* aired on Dec. 20, 2005.

Heaven Is for Real (TriStar Pictures Roth Films, 2014) is a movie where the son of a pastor claims to have visited heaven.

Mahalia Jackson's 1954 song, "Walk Over God's Heaven," in which she sings, "Everybody's talkin' 'bout heav'n, ain't going there."

"America's Changing Religious Landscape." The Pew Research Centers 2014 Religious Landscape Study, accessible at https://www.pewforum.org/2015/05/12/americas-changing-religious-landscape/.

Baker, Stephen. "Queen Victoria's Conversion—Being Sure of Eternal Life!" *Finding the Missing Peace* (Feb. 10, 2017, accessible at http://www.findingthemissing-peace.co.uk/2017/02/queen-victorias-conversion-be-ing-sure.html).

Gibbs, Nancy and Michael Duffy. *The Preacher and the Presidents: Billy Graham in the White House* (original copyright 2007; reprinted by permission of Center Street, an imprint of Hachette Book Group, Inc., 2008).

Evangelist Arthur Blessitt recorded his meeting with George W. Bush on April 3, 1984, Midland, Texas, in his official website's blog entry "Praying with George W. Bush" (accessible at https://www.blessitt.com/praying-with-george-w-bush/).

Whitney Houston's last interview with Diane Sawyer was a primetime special in 2002, now available on *Dailymotion* at https://www.dailymotion.com/video/x2hhajc.

St. Augustine quote found on *Catholic Link* (https://catholic-link.org/quotes/st-augustine-quotes-you-have-made-us-for-yourself-o-lord/).

Chapter 2

Scriptures

2 Kings 5
Ephesians 2:8–9
Matthew 9:13
John 19:10
1 Timothy 1:15–16

References

The story of former white supremist Christian Picciolini was aired on *NPR* with host Dave Davies on Jan. 18, 2018, "A Former Neo-Nazi Explains Why Hate Drew Him In—And How He Got Out," audio and transcript available at https://www.npr.org/transcripts/578745514.

Ray C. Stedman writes about Rev. Billy Graham and Sir Winston Churchill in *God's Final Word* (Our Daily Bread Publishing, 1991), chapter 16.

Roper, David. "A Chuckle in the Darkness." *Our Daily Bread* devotional. Feb. 28, 2017.

Chapter 3

Scripture

Romans 6:23
John 3:16
1 Timothy 2:4
2 Peter 3:9
Matthew 20:28
Matthew 1:21
Luke 2:10

Isaiah 9:6

Romans 10:9

John 20:29

2 Corinthians 5:7

Ephesians 2:8–9

Romans 3:23

John 11:25

Romans 6:23

References

Annabel Beam and Miracles from Heaven (June 15, 2016).

Chapter 4

Scriptures

John 14:1–6
Acts 4:12
Acts 10:43
Acts 16:31
1 John 5:11
1 John 5:12
John 3:36
John 6:28

John 6:38

John 6:40

John 10:28

Isaiah 43:11

John 3:16

Romans 10:9

2 Timothy 1:12

1 John 5:12–13

Matthew 3:17

Matthew 17:5

Mark 9:7

Romans 5:7–8

1 Corinthians 15:3–8

John 20:24–31

Acts 1:3

References

Lucado, Max. *Grace for the Moment: Inspirational Thoughts for Each Day of the Year*, April 16: "The Only Path." Thomas Nelson, 2000.

Chapter 5

Scriptures

Genesis 2:9

Genesis 2:16–17

Acts 17:26

Romans 5:12

1 Corinthians 15:22

Rom 6:23

John 3:16

John 3:3

2 Corinthians 5:17

John 3:3

1 Corinthians 15:49

1 John 1:12–13

Galatians 3:26

John 14:26

Acts 2:38

Ephesians 2:4

Reference

Hymn: "What Can Wash away My Sins? Nothing but the
Blood of Jesus."

Chapter 6

Scriptures

Romans 3:24–30

Galatians 3:26

Hebrews 11:6

Jeremiah 29:13

Deuteronomy 4:29

Acts 17:22–31

Romans 4:19

John 6:38–40

Ephesians 3:18–19

Isaiah 26:3

Matthew 28:20

Mark 2:4

Matthew 19

Matthew 2

Matthew 6:33

Psalm 34:8

James 4:8

James 1:17

Ephesians 4:22–24

Philippians 2:5

Reference

Hymn: "I Don't Know Why Jesus Loves Me."

Chapter 7

Scriptures

John 11:25

Mark 2:17

Ephesians 4:30

Ephesians 1:14

2 Corinthians 1:22

2 Corinthians 5:5

Romans 7:18

Romans 7:21

Galatians 5:17

Romans 6:23

Romans 5:8

Philippians 1:6

1 John 1:8

John 10:28

Romans 8:1

Romans 8:35

Matthew 28:20

Hebrews 13:5

References

Colonial Penn Life Insurance. colonialpenn.com.

Mart DeHaan, founder of the Radio Bible Class and coeditor of monthly devotional guide *Our Daily Bread*, wrote *Following Jesus: Relationship or Religion?* for the *Discovery Series* (Our Daily Bread Ministries, 2014).

Chapter 8

Scriptures

Matthew 16:24
Mark 8:34
Luke 9:23
Romans 12:2
John 16:33
Matthew 5:45
Colossians 2:8
2 Peter 3:17–18

Reference

The documentary *Holy Hell*, directed and produced by Will Allen, premiered during the Sundance Film Festival in 2016 and was later picked up and aired by CNN.

Chapter 9

Scriptures

> Revelations 21:1
> Philippians 2:10–11
> Matthew 24:35

Reference

Yale University Professor of Literature William Lyon Phelps (1865–1943). Quote compiled in Tony Cooke's "Great Statements Concerning the Bible" (https://tonycooke. org/stories-and-illustrations/great-statements/).

ABOUT THE AUTHOR

Patricia Palmer White, a native of Newport News, Virginia, is the widow of Pastor Calvin D. White from Louisville, Kentucky, where they served as pastor and first lady of the Beargrass Missionary Baptist Church for eighteen years. Returning to Virginia to care for her ailing mother, Patricia Palmer White became the first lady of the Union Bethel Baptist Church in Chesapeake, where Rev. White pastored for seven years until he was called home to glory. Her role as wife to Pastor White, mother of Kevin and Jaci, grandmother of eight, and great-grandmother of fourteen did not hinder her in her duties as first lady. She faithfully served as youth director, Sunday school teacher, youth Bible study teacher, Vacation Bible School study teacher, Sonbeam choir director, and program director of the church drama group. She is passionate about the children knowing the Lord and how to handle His Word. Her personal relationship with Jesus Christ keeps her aware of His abiding presence. First Lady White's favorite scripture is Psalm 16:8: "I have set the Lord always before me. Because He is at my right hand, I will not be shaken" (NIV). Her mantra is: "Thank God for Jesus."